# FAST FACT

- Spanish is the second most widely spoken language in the world
- Mexico is the largest Spanish-speaking country
- In 1492, Antonio de Nebrija was the author of the first Spanish grammar book
- The vowel "e" is the most used letter in the Spanish language
- Spanish can sometime have upside down exclamation marks and question marks at the front of a sentence
- Because Spanish and English both have Latin roots - there are a lot of common vocabulary in Spanish just like in the English language
- If you find any words that are the same in both languages they are referred to as English-Spanish cognates
- A 400-word document in English is usually 450-500 words in Spanish - text in Spanish is about 15 – 30% longer
- Spanish has two names - Castellano and Español

TIP: DOWNLOAD THE FREE GOOGLE TRANSLATE APP TO HELP YOU WITH THIS WORKBOOK.

SCORE:_____

DATE_____

# Definite vs. Indefinite Articles

What is the difference between a definite and indefinite article in Spanish?
EXPLAIN HERE:

Look at the words below and fill in the answers to the table below. Follow the example. Some answers are already there to help you.

| Palabra | ¿En español? | Singular/Plural (escribe el opuesto) |
|---|---|---|
| Ej. The book | El libro. | Los libros. |
| 1. The teacher | | |
| 2. Some pencils | | Un lápiz |
| 3. A student desk | | |
| 4. The door | | |
| 5. Some books | Unos libros | |
| 6. A class | | |
| 7. The shoes | | |
| 8. A clock | | |
| 9. A shoe | | Unos zapatos |

| | | |
|---|---|---|
| 10. The pencil | | |
| 11. Some chairs | | Una silla |
| 12. The lights | | |
| 13. A computer | | Unas computadoras |
| 14. The pencil sharpener | | |
| 15. A chalkboard | | |
| 16. Some girls | Unas chicas | |
| 17. A chalkboard eraser | | |
| 18. Some students | | |
| 19. The table | | |
| 20. The windows | La ventana | |

Date: _____

# Spanish Nouns

Whenever the Spanish word is a noun, be sure to start with the definite article (el, la, los, las).

el = the (masculine singular)
los = the (masculine plural)
la = the (feminine singular)
las = the (feminine plural)

**Masculine Examples:**

el libro = the book
los perros = the dogs

**Feminine Examples:**

la vaca = the cow
las playas = the beaches

### FILL IN THE CHART BELOW WITH YOUR OWN EXAMPLES.

| 3 Masculine Examples: (el) | 3 Feminine Examples: (la) |
|---|---|
| el: | la: |
| el: | la: |
| el: | la: |

| 3 Masculine Examples: (los) | 3 Feminine Examples: (las) |
|---|---|
| los: | las: |
| los: | las: |
| los: | las: |

| 4 Masculine Examples: (el & los) | 4 Feminine Examples: (la & las) |
|---|---|
| el: | la: |
| el: | la: |
| los: | las: |
| los: | las: |

| 2 Masculine & Feminine Examples: (el & la) | 2 Feminine & Masculine Examples: (la & los) |
|---|---|
| el: | la: |
| la: | los: |

# TIME

**To ask what time it is in Spanish you simply say:** <u>¿Qué hora es?</u>

<u>Telling Time (:00-:30)</u>

### For <u>all time periods except one o'clock</u> you say: Son las + the number representing the hour.

<u>Ejemplo:</u>

Son las dos de la tarde. / It's 2 o'clock in the afternoon.

Son las cinco de la tarde. / It's 5 o'clock in the afternoon.

### For <u>additional minutes</u> past the whole hour, <u>add them on</u> to the end.

<u>Ejemplo:</u>

Son las cinco y diez de la mañana. / It's 5:10 in the morning. Son

las cuatro y veinte de la tarde. / It's 4:20 in the afternoon.

### For the <u>one o'clock</u> hour, use <u>"Es la"</u> instead of "Son las."

<u>Ejemplo:</u>

Es la una de la tarde. / It's one o'clock in the afternoon.

Es la una y veinticinco de la tarde. / It's 1:25 in the afternoon.

### For <u>:15 after</u> use the expression <u>"y cuarto."</u> For <u>:30 after</u> you use the expression <u>"y media."</u>

<u>Ejemplo:</u>

Son las dos y cuarto de la tarde. / It's 2:15 in the afternoon.

Es la una y media de la mañana. / It's 1:30 in the morning.

**Don't forget to be specific about morning, afternoon, and evening hours using "de la mañana, de la tarde, de la noche".**

Telling time :30-:00

## For all time periods except one o'clock you say:
## Son las + the number representing the hour.

Ejemplo:

Son las dos de la tarde./It's 2 o'clock in the afternoon.

Son las cinco de la tarde./ It's 5 o'clock in the afternoon.

## For additional minutes past the half hour, you must round up to the next full hour, and subtract the minutes you "fudged." Use "menos" instead of "y."

Ejemplo:

It's 5:50 p.m. → Son las seis menos diez de la tarde.

It's 7:35 a.m. → Son las ocho menos veinticinco de la mañana.

## For :15 to the hour subtract using the expression "menos cuarto"

It's 2:45 p.m. → Son las tres menos cuarto de la tarde.

It's 9:45p.m. → Son las diez menos cuarto de la noche.

# Time, Days, and Months

| Monday = el lunes | Tuesday = el martes | Wednesday = el miércoles | Thursday = el jueves |
| Friday = el viernes | Saturday = el sábado | Sunday = el domingo | January = enero |
| February = febrero | March = marzo | April = abril | May = mayo |
| June = junio | July = julio | August = agosto | September = septiembre |
| October = octubre | November = noviembre | December = diciembre | century = el siglo |

| | | | |
|---|---|---|---|
| decade<br>= la década | year<br>= el año | month<br>= el mes | week<br>= la semana |
| day<br>= el día | the day before yesterday =<br>anteayer | yesterday = ayer | today<br>= hoy |
| tomorrow<br>= mañana | the day after tomorrow<br>= pasado mañana | dawn<br>= la madrugada | midnight<br>= la medianoche |
| noon<br>= el mediodía | afternoon<br>= la tarde | evening, night =<br>la noche | |

Did you know that months of the year in English and Spanish are similar because they come from the age of the Roman Empire.

Name: _____

Date: _____

# Match The Pairs

Learn how to *look up* words in a *Spanish-English dictionary* or online. Draw a line or write corresponding letter.

|  | |  | |  | |
|---|---|---|---|---|---|
| 1 | ☐ | Gracias! | | Please (generally used at the end of a sentence) | A |
| 2 | ☐ | ¡Muchas gracias! | | Sorry! (to apologize for a mistake) | B |
| 3 | ☐ | ¡De nada! | | Why? | C |
| 4 | ☐ | Por favor | | How? | D |
| 5 | ☐ | ¡Perdon! | | Thank you very much! | E |
| 6 | ☐ | ¡Lo siento! | | When? | F |
| 7 | ☐ | ¿Qué…? | | Who? | G |
| 8 | ☐ | ¿Quién…? | | Which? | H |
| 9 | ☐ | ¿Cuándo…? | | Thank you! | I |
| 10 | ☐ | ¿Dónde…? | | You're welcome! / No problem! | J |
| 11 | ☐ | ¿Por qué…? | | Where? | K |
| 12 | ☐ | ¿Cuál? | | Excuse me! | L |
| 13 | ☐ | ¿Cómo…? | | What? | M |

Write 3 sentences using Spanish words or phrases from above:

_____

_____

_____

# Greetings

| Señor = Mr. | Señora = Mrs. | Señorita = Miss. | Don = Sir |
|---|---|---|---|
| Doña = Madam | What is your name?<br><br>= ¿Cómo se llama usted? | How are you?<br><br>= ¿Cómo está usted? | I am fine.<br><br>= Estoy bien. |
| And you?<br><br>= ¿y usted? | Pleased to meet you.<br><br>= Mucho gusto. | Goodbye.<br><br>= Adiós. | See you later.<br><br>= Hasta luego. |
| See you tomorrow.<br><br>= Hasta mañana. | | | |

Write 3 sentences using Spanish words or phrases from above:

............................................................................................................................

............................................................................................................................

............................................................................................................................

| | | | |
|---|---|---|---|
| Good morning. = Buenos días. | Good afternoon. = Buenas tardes. | Good evening. = Buenas noches. | Hello, my name is John. = Hola, me llamo Juan. |
| What is your name? = ¿Cómo se llama usted? | How are you? = ¿Cómo está usted? | I am fine. = Estoy bien. | Nice to meet you. = Mucho gusto. |
| Goodbye. = Adiós. | See you later. = Hasta luego. | Excuse me. = Con permiso. OR Perdóname | Please. = Por favor. |
| Thank you. = Gracías. | I'm sorry. = Lo siento. | Bless you. = Salud. | You are welcome = De nada. |
| How much does it cost? = ¿Cuánto cuesta? | How many are there? = ¿Cuántos hay? | There are many. = Hay muchos. | Do you want to buy this? = ¿Quiere comprarlo usted? |

| | | | |
|---|---|---|---|
| What time is it? <br> = <br> ¿Qué hora es? | Yes. <br> = <br> Sí. | No. <br> = <br> No. | I do not understand. <br> = <br> Yo no comprendo. |
| Would you speak slower, please. <br> = <br> Por favor, habla mas despacio. | Who? <br> = <br> ¿Quièn? | Why? <br> = <br> ¿Por què? | |

Write 8 sentences using Spanish words or phrases from above:

................................................................................................................................................

................................................................................................................................................

................................................................................................................................................

................................................................................................................................................

................................................................................................................................................

................................................................................................................................................

................................................................................................................................................

................................................................................................................................................

Date: _____

# Everyday English Greetings

Download the free **Google Translate** app. Select the conversation option via the app. Speak each English word or phrase into your device. You'll *hear* the *translation* spoken aloud in Spanish as well written in Spanish. Write down the Spanish version for each below.

- ❖ Hello. How do you do?

  (You can write on one or both lines)
  - _____
  - _____

- ❖ Good night! See you tomorrow.
  - _____
  - _____

- ❖ Good afternoon, Ms. Jones.
  - _____
  - _____

- ❖ Good evening, Kelly.
  - _____
  - _____

- ❖ How have you been?
  - _____
  - _____

- ❖ Hello, Matt. How are you?
  - _____
  - _____

- ❖ Hello, Amanda! How are you doing?
  - _____
  - _____

- ❖ Hi, Michel. How's it going?
  - _____
  - _____

- ❖ It was nice to meet you. Good night!
  - _____
  - _____

- ❖ Good morning, Mr. Houston.
  - _____
  - _____

- ❖ Good morning, John.
  - _____
  - _____

- ❖ Nice to meet you, Mr. White.
  - _____
  - _____

- ❖ I've been busy working a lot. How about you?
  - _____
  - _____

- ❖ Hi, Monica. Nice to see you!
  - _____
  - _____

- ❖ Fine, thanks. And you?
  - _____
  - _____

- ❖ Great! How about you?
  - _____
  - _____

- Hello, Veronica. Nice to see you there.
  - _____
  - _____

- Hey, John! Long-time no see. How are you?
  - _____
  - _____

- Hi, Chris. How's it going?
  - _____
  - _____

- I haven't seen you for ages.
  - _____
  - _____

- Well, it was great to see you. Have a good day.
  - _____
  - _____

- I'm fine, thanks! What's new?
  - _____
  - _____

- Good thanks.
  - _____
  - _____

- Yes, it's been a while.
  - _____
  - _____

# Numbers

| | | | |
|---|---|---|---|
| 1 - uno | 2 - dos | 3 - tres | 4 - cuatro |
| 5 - cinco | 6 - seis | 7 - siete | 8 - ocho |
| 9 - nueve | 10 - diez | 11 - once | 12 - doce |
| 13 - trece | 14 - catorce | 15 - quince | 16 - dieciséis |
| 17 - diecisiete | 18 - dieciocho | 19 - diecinueve | 20 - veinte |

| | | | |
|---|---|---|---|
| 21 - veintiuno | 22 - veintidós | 23 - veintitrés | 24 - veinticuatro |
| 25 - veinticinco | 26 - veintiséis | 27 - veintisiete | 28 - veintiocho |
| 29 - veintinueve | 30 - treinta | 31 - treinta y uno | 32 - treinta y dos |
| 33 - treinta y tres | 40 - cuarenta | 41 - cuarenta y uno | 42 - cuarenta y dos |
| 50 - cincuenta | 60 - sesenta | 70 - setenta | 80 - ochenta |

| 90 - noventa | 100 - cien | 200 - doscientos | 300 - trescientos |
|---|---|---|---|
| 400 - cuatrocientos | 500 - quinientos | 600 - seiscientos | 700 - setecientos |
| 800 - ochocientos | 900 - novecientos | 1.000 - mil | 2.000 - dos mil |

# Colors

| | | | |
|---|---|---|---|
| blue = azul | brown = marrón | black = negro | green = verde |
| grey = gris | orange = anaranjado | pink = rosa | red = rojo |
| silvery = plateado | white = blanco | yellow = amarillo | gold = dorado |
| purple = morado | sky blue = azúl cielo | light blue = celeste | navy blue = azul marino |
| turquoise = turquesa | violet = violeta | dark = moreno | lilac = lila |

| tan = café claro | transparent = transparente | clear, light = claro | |

# Common Stuff We Say

Date: _____

Download the free **Google Translate** app. Select the conversation option via the app. Speak each English word or phrase into your device. You'll *hear* the *translation* spoken aloud in Spanish as well written in Spanish. Write down the Spanish version for each below.

- I love you.
    - _____
    - _____

- You make me happy.
    - _____
    - _____

- Thank you.
    - _____
    - _____

- I was wrong.
    - _____
    - _____

- Will you forgive me?
    - _____
    - _____

- You are beautiful.
    - _____
    - _____

- I'm feeling angry.
    - _____
    - _____

- I appreciate you!
    - _____
    - _____

- I like that.
    - _____
    - _____

- Please.
    - _____
    - _____

- You're welcome.
    - _____
    - _____

- You are right.
    - _____
    - _____

- You are hurting my feelings.
    - _____
    - _____

- That looks nice on you.
    - _____
    - _____

- Are you upset?
    - _____
    - _____

- I'm tired.
    - _____
    - _____

- Will you help me?
    - _____
    - _____

- What is your address?
    - _____
    - _____

- What's your name?
    - _____
    - _____

- What size is that?
    - _____
    - _____

- That's a good idea.
    - _____
    - _____

- I am a boy.
    - _____
    - _____

- How old are you?
    - _____
    - _____

- It is wonderful.
    - _____
    - _____

- What time is it?
    - _____
    - _____

- What did he tell you?
    - _____
    - _____

- It's getting dark.
    - _____
    - _____

- Can I help you?
    - _____
    - _____

- What are those?
    - _____
    - _____

- What color is this?
    - _____
    - _____

- What day is today?
    - _____
    - _____

- I am a girl.
    - _____
    - _____

- Who are you?
    - _____
    - _____

- Where are you?
    - _____
    - _____

- I'm thirsty.
    - _____
    - _____

- Are you sure?
    - _____
    - _____

- Don't get excited!
    - _____
    - _____

- Do you understand?
    - _____
    - _____

# Match The Pairs

Name: _____

Date: _____

Learn how to *look up* words in a *Spanish-English dictionary* or online. Draw a line or write corresponding letter.

|  |  | |  |  |
|---|---------|---|---------|--------|
| 1 | Sí | | My Spanish is bad | A |
| 2 | No | | Never | B |
| 3 | Tal vez | | Maybe | C |
| 4 | Siempre | | I don't speak Spanish | D |
| 5 | Nunca | | No problem! | E |
| 6 | Claro | | Yes | F |
| 7 | ¡Sin problema! | | Always | G |
| 8 | No entiendo | | I don't know! | H |
| 9 | No (lo) sé | | I have no idea! | I |
| 10 | No tengo ni idea | | No | J |
| 11 | No hablo español | | I don't understand! | K |
| 12 | Estoy perdido | | Of course | L |
| 13 | Mi español es malo | | I'm lost | M |

| ¿Qué hora tienes? — What time is it? | ¿De dónde viene? — Where are you from? | ¿Dónde vives? — Where do you live? | ¿Puede ayudarme? — Can you help me? |
|---|---|---|---|
| ¿Podría ayudarle? — Can I help you? | ¿Cuánto cuesta eso? — How much does it cost? | ¿Qué hora tienes? — What time is it? | ¿Entiende? — Do you understand? |
| ¡Puede repetirlo! — Can you say that again? | ¿Qué significa [word]? — What does [word] mean? | ¿Puedes hablar más despacio? — Can you speak slowly? | ¿Dónde puedo encontrar un taxi? — Where can I find a taxi? |

Write 3 sentences using Spanish words or phrases from above:

_____

_____

_____

_____

_____

_____

# Adjectives

| hot (temperature) = caliente | hot (spicy) = picante | cold = frío(a) | yummy/delicious = rico(a) |
|---|---|---|---|
| bitter = amargo(a) | sweet = dulce | perfect = perfecto(a) | frozen = congelado(a) |
| grilled/roasted = asado(a) | fried = frito(a) | boiled = hervido(a) | gross = asqueroso(a) |
| good-looking = guapo(a) | cute/pretty = lindo(a) | pretty = bonito(a) | beautiful = hermoso(a) |
| precious = precioso(a) | thin = delgado(a) | fat = gordo(a) | weak = débil |

| | | | |
|---|---|---|---|
| strong<br>=<br>fuerte | tall<br>=<br>alto(a) | short<br>=<br>bajo(a) | nice<br>=<br>simpático(a) |
| mean<br>=<br>antipático(a) | friendly/polite<br>=<br>amable | funny<br>= gracioso(a) | boring<br>= aburrido(a) |
| fun<br>=<br>divertido(a) | warm/endearing<br>= cariñoso(a) | weird/odd<br>=<br>raro(a) | fierce<br>=<br>feroz |
| creative<br>=<br>creativo(a) | brave<br>=<br>valiente | crazy<br>=<br>loco(a) | |

Write 3 sentences using Spanish words or phrases from above:

.................................................................................................................................................

.................................................................................................................................................

.................................................................................................................................................

# Match The Pairs - Spanish Adjectives

Name: _____

Date: _____

Learn how to *look up* words in a *Spanish-English dictionary or online.* Write corresponding letter(s) for the correct answer.

|  | |  | |  |  |
|---|---|---|---|---|---|
| 1 | ☐ | Abierto(a) | | Bitter | A |
| 2 | ☐ | Aburrido(a) | | Difficult, hard | B |
| 3 | ☐ | Afortunado(a) | | Worried | C |
| 4 | ☐ | Agradable | | Excited | D |
| 5 | ☐ | Alto(a) | | Young | E |
| 6 | ☐ | Amable | | Fast | F |
| 7 | ☐ | Amargo(a) | | Near | G |
| 8 | ☐ | Amigable | | Excellent | H |
| 9 | ☐ | Ancho(a) | | Thin, slim, lean | I |
| 10 | ☐ | Apretado | | Short | J |
| 11 | ☐ | Bajo(a) | | Thick | K |
| 12 | ☐ | Barato(a) | | Wrong | L |
| 13 | ☐ | Blando(a) | | Loud | M |
| 14 | ☐ | Bonito(a) | | Long | N |
| 15 | ☐ | Bueno(a) | | Hard | O |
| 16 | ☐ | Caliente | | Safe | P |
| 17 | ☐ | Caro(a) | | Stingy | Q |

| # | | Spanish | | English | Code |
|---|---|---|---|---|---|
| 18 | ☐ | Cerca | | Quiet | R |
| 19 | ☐ | Cerrado(a) | | Closed, shut | S |
| 20 | ☐ | Correcto(a) | | Lucky | T |
| 21 | ☐ | Corto(a) | | FALSE | U |
| 22 | ☐ | Delgado(a) | | Far | V |
| 23 | ☐ | Débil | | Clean | W |
| 24 | ☐ | Desafortunado(a) | | Dead | X |
| 25 | ☐ | Desagradable | | Many | Y |
| 26 | ☐ | Difícil | | Unpleasant | Z |
| 27 | ☐ | Divertido(a) | | TRUE | AA |
| 28 | ☐ | Dulce | | Right, correct | AB |
| 29 | ☐ | Duro(a) | | Low | AC |
| 30 | ☐ | Educado(a) | | Slow | AD |
| 31 | ☐ | Emocionado(a) | | Interesting | AE |
| 32 | ☐ | Enojado(a) | | Heavy | AF |
| 33 | ☐ | Equivocado(a) | | Shy | AG |
| 34 | ☐ | Estrecho(a) | | Stupid | AH |
| 35 | ☐ | Estúpido(a) | | Cold | AI |
| 36 | ☐ | Excelente | | Late | AJ |
| 37 | ☐ | Fácil | | Dangerous | AK |
| 38 | ☐ | Falso(a) | | Early | AL |
| 39 | ☐ | Feliz | | Intelligent | AM |

| # | | Spanish | | English | Code |
|---|---|---|---|---|---|
| 40 | ☐ | Feo(a) | | Friendly | AN |
| 41 | ☐ | Fino(a) | | High, tall | AO |
| 42 | ☐ | Frio(a) | | Nice, pretty | AP |
| 43 | ☐ | Fuerte | | Ugly | AQ |
| 44 | ☐ | Generoso(a) | | Dirty | AR |
| 45 | ☐ | Gordo(a) | | Light | AS |
| 46 | ☐ | Grande | | Thin | AT |
| 47 | ☐ | Grueso(a) | | Sweet | AU |
| 48 | ☐ | Hermoso(a) | | Friendly | AV |
| 49 | ☐ | Holgado(a) | | Rude | AW |
| 50 | ☐ | Importante | | Expensive | AX |
| 51 | ☐ | Inteligente | | Open | AY |
| 52 | ☐ | Interesante | | Rich | AZ |
| 53 | ☐ | Inútil | | Beautiful | BA |
| 54 | ☐ | Joven | | Loose, baggy | BB |
| 55 | ☐ | Largo(a) | | Pleasant | BC |
| 56 | ☐ | Lejos | | Dark | BD |
| 57 | ☐ | Lento(a) | | Important | BE |
| 58 | ☐ | Ligero(a) | | Wide | BF |
| 59 | ☐ | Limpio(a) | | Short | BG |
| 60 | ☐ | Lleno(a) | | Deep | BH |
| 61 | ☐ | Loco(a) | | Hot | BI |

| # | | Spanish | | English | Code |
|---|---|---|---|---|---|
| 62 | ☐ | Luminoso(a) | | Alive | BJ |
| 63 | ☐ | Mal educado(a) | | Few | BK |
| 64 | ☐ | Malo(a) | | Fun | BL |
| 65 | ☐ | Mojado(a) | | Useful | BM |
| 66 | ☐ | Muchos(as) | | Strong | BN |
| 67 | ☐ | Muerto(a) | | Angry | BO |
| 68 | ☐ | Nuevo(a) | | Unlucky | BP |
| 69 | ☐ | Oscuro(a) | | Poor | BQ |
| 70 | ☐ | Peligroso(a) | | Cheap | BR |
| 71 | ☐ | Pequeño(a) | | Shallow | BS |
| 72 | ☐ | Pesado(a) | | Generous | BT |
| 73 | ☐ | Petizo(a) | | Boring | BU |
| 74 | ☐ | Pobre | | Sad | BV |
| 75 | ☐ | Pocos(as) | | Bright | BW |
| 76 | ☐ | Preocupado(a) | | Narrow | BX |
| 77 | ☐ | Profundo(a) | | Dry | BY |
| 78 | ☐ | Rápido(a) | | Tight | BZ |
| 79 | ☐ | Relajado(a) | | Happy | CA |
| 80 | ☐ | Rico(a) | | Old | CB |
| 81 | ☐ | Ruidoso(a) | | Crazy | CC |
| 82 | ☐ | Seco(a) | | Bad | CD |
| 83 | ☐ | Seguro(a) | | Fat | CE |

| # | | Spanish | | English | Code |
|---|---|---|---|---|---|
| 84 | ☐ | Sin importancia | | Empty | CF |
| 85 | ☐ | Sucio(a) | | Wet | CG |
| 86 | ☐ | Superficial | | Big | CH |
| 87 | ☐ | Tacaño(a) | | Relaxed | CI |
| 88 | ☐ | Tarde | | Useless | CJ |
| 89 | ☐ | Temprano | | Full | CK |
| 90 | ☐ | Tímido(a) | | New | CL |
| 91 | ☐ | Tranquilo(a) | | Unimportant | CM |
| 92 | ☐ | Triste | | Soft | CN |
| 93 | ☐ | Útil | | Easy | CO |
| 94 | ☐ | Vacío(a) | | Good | CP |
| 95 | ☐ | Verdadero(a) | | Weak | CQ |
| 96 | ☐ | Viejo(a) | | Small | CR |
| 97 | ☐ | Vivo(a) | | Polite | CS |

Write 5 sentences using Spanish words or phrases from above:

# Family

| | | | |
|---|---|---|---|
| grandmother = abuela | grandma = abuelita | grandpa = abuelito | grandfather = abuelo |
| grandparents = abuelos | wedding = boda | close friend = compadre | brother-in-law = cuñado |
| wife = esposa | family = familia | identical twin = gemelo | sister = hermana |
| younger sister = hermana menor | step-brother = hermanastro | step-brother = hermanastro | brother = hermano |
| daughter = hija | son = hijo | orphan = huérfano | step-mother = madrastra |

| mother = madre | godmother = madrina | mom = mamá | mommy = mami |
| husband = marido | twin = mellizo | granddaughter = nieta | grandson = nieto |
| nickname for godmother = nina | nickname for godfather = nino | bride, fiancé, girlfriend = novia | groom, fiancé, boyfriend = novio |
| daughter-in-law = nuera | step-father = padrastro | father = padre | parents = padres |
| godfather = padrino | godparents = padrinos | dad = papá | daddy = papi |

| relatives = parientes | cousin (female) = prima | cousin (male) = primo | first cousin (male) = primo hermano |
|---|---|---|---|
| niece = sobrina | nephew = sobrino | mother-in-law = suegra | father-in-law = suegro |
| aunt = tía | uncle = tío | neighbors = vecinos | widow = viuda |
| widower = viudo | son-in-law = yerno | | |

Write 4 sentences using Spanish words or phrases from above:

# Match The Pairs - Spanish Adjectives

Name: _____

Date: _____

Learn how to *look up* words in a *Spanish-English dictionary* or online. Write corresponding letter(s) for the correct answer.

|  | |  | |  |  |
|---|---|---|---|---|---|
| 1 | ☐ | Bad | | Frío | A |
| 2 | ☐ | Beautiful | | Delgado | B |
| 3 | ☐ | Big | | Difícil | C |
| 4 | ☐ | Bitter | | Oscuro | D |
| 5 | ☐ | Boring | | Joven | E |
| 6 | ☐ | Calm | | Complicado | F |
| 7 | ☐ | Cheap | | Sucio | G |
| 8 | ☐ | Clear | | Cortés | H |
| 9 | ☐ | Cold | | Modesto | I |
| 10 | ☐ | Complicated | | Salado | J |
| 11 | ☐ | Curious | | Pobre | K |
| 12 | ☐ | Dark | | Corto | L |
| 13 | ☐ | Difficult | | Hermoso | M |
| 14 | ☐ | Diligent | | Rico | N |
| 15 | ☐ | Dirty | | Seco | O |
| 16 | ☐ | Dry | | Gordo | P |
| 17 | ☐ | Easy | | Poco | Q |

| # | | English | | Spanish | Code |
|---|---|---|---|---|---|
| 18 | ☐ | Empty | | Aburrido | R |
| 19 | ☐ | Entertaining | | Divertido | S |
| 20 | ☐ | Expensive | | Malo | T |
| 21 | ☐ | Fair | | Honesto | U |
| 22 | ☐ | Fat | | Largo | V |
| 23 | ☐ | Few | | Débil | W |
| 24 | ☐ | Full | | Perezoso | X |
| 25 | ☐ | Good | | Fuerte | Y |
| 26 | ☐ | Happy | | Ancho | Z |
| 27 | ☐ | Hard | | Alto | AA |
| 28 | ☐ | Healthy | | Claro | AB |
| 29 | ☐ | Honest | | Puro | AC |
| 30 | ☐ | Interesting | | Lento | AD |
| 31 | ☐ | Lazy | | Caliente | AE |
| 32 | ☐ | Lean | | Bajo | AF |
| 33 | ☐ | Long | | Tranquilo | AG |
| 34 | ☐ | Low | | Duro | AH |
| 35 | ☐ | Modest | | Grande | AI |
| 36 | ☐ | Much | | Nervioso | AJ |
| 37 | ☐ | Narrow | | Barato | AK |
| 38 | ☐ | Nervous | | Bueno | AL |
| 39 | ☐ | New | | Enfermo | AM |

| # | | English | | Spanish | Code |
|---|---|---|---|---|---|
| 40 | ☐ | Old | | Sencillo | AN |
| 41 | ☐ | Polite | | Antiguo, Viejo | AO |
| 42 | ☐ | Poor | | Amargo | AP |
| 43 | ☐ | Pretty | | Lleno | AQ |
| 44 | ☐ | Pure | | Fácil | AR |
| 45 | ☐ | Quick | | Pequeño | AS |
| 46 | ☐ | Rich | | Cansado | AT |
| 47 | ☐ | Sad | | Feo | AU |
| 48 | ☐ | Salty | | Flaco | AV |
| 49 | ☐ | Short | | Sano | AW |
| 50 | ☐ | Sick | | Injusto | AX |
| 51 | ☐ | Simple | | Alegre, Feliz | AY |
| 52 | ☐ | Slow | | Triste | AZ |
| 53 | ☐ | Small | | Mucho | BA |
| 54 | ☐ | Strong | | Justo | BB |
| 55 | ☐ | Stupid | | Curioso | BC |
| 56 | ☐ | Sweet | | Aplicado | BD |
| 57 | ☐ | Tall | | Vacío | BE |
| 58 | ☐ | Thick | | Interesante | BF |
| 59 | ☐ | Thin | | Caro | BG |
| 60 | ☐ | Tired | | Rápido | BH |
| 61 | ☐ | Ugly | | Estrecho | BI |

|  | | | | | |
|---|---|---|---|---|---|
| 62 | ☐ | Unfair | Nuevo | | BJ |
| 63 | ☐ | Warm | Guapo | | BK |
| 64 | ☐ | Weak | Dulce | | BL |
| 65 | ☐ | Wide | Grueso | | BM |
| 66 | ☐ | Young | Tonto | | BN |

Write 10 sentences using Spanish words or phrases from above:

# Match The Phrases

Name: _____

Date: _____

Learn how to *look up* words in a *Spanish-English dictionary* or online. Draw a line or write corresponding letter.

|  | |  | |  |  |
|---|---|---|---|---|---|
| 1 | ☐ | Can I help you? | | ¿Cuánto cuesta? | A |
| 2 | ☐ | Anything else? | | ¿Eso es todo? | B |
| 3 | ☐ | Is that all? | | ¿Cuánto (le) debo? | C |
| 4 | ☐ | How much does it cost? | | Llámele en cinco minutos. | D |
| 5 | ☐ | How much do I owe you? | | Quisiera comprar ... | E |
| 6 | ☐ | I would like to buy ... | | ¿Con quién hablo? | F |
| 7 | ☐ | Where can I buy a ... | | Se ha equivocado. | G |
| 8 | ☐ | I'd like a kilo of apple, please. | | ¿Tiene otro / Hay otro? | H |
| 9 | ☐ | Three cans of beer, please. | | ¿Puedo probármela / -lo? | I |
| 10 | ☐ | One pack, please. | | ¿Puede cambiármelo? | J |
| 11 | ☐ | A bit more / less. | | ¿Tiene otro más barato? | K |
| 12 | ☐ | I need a stamp, too. | | No me gusta el color / la tela. | L |
| 13 | ☐ | Would you give me a bag? | | Espere, por favor. | M |
| 14 | ☐ | Would you change it for me? | | ¿Dónde puedo comprar un ...? | N |
| 15 | ☐ | Do you have ...? | | ¿Qué ... tiene? | O |
| 16 | ☐ | What ...do you have? | | ¿Qué desea? | P |
| 17 | ☐ | Is there another one? | | ¿Algo más? | Q |

| | | |
|---|---|---|
| 18 | ☐ | Is there a cheaper one? |
| 19 | ☐ | Can I try it on? |
| 20 | ☐ | I don't like the color / the fabric. |
| 21 | ☐ | Who is that? |
| 22 | ☐ | Hold on, please. |
| 23 | ☐ | Call him/her later. |
| 24 | ☐ | Call him/her in five minutes. |
| 25 | ☐ | You've called the wrong number. |

| | |
|---|---|
| Un poco más / menos. | R |
| ¿Tiene ...? | S |
| Tres latas de cerveza, por favor. | T |
| ¿Puede darme una bolsa? | U |
| Llámele más tarde. | V |
| Déme un paquete. | W |
| Déme, por favor, un kilo de manzanas. | X |
| Necesito un sello también. | Y |

# PHRASES

| I don't mind. = Me da lo mismo. | I don't know. = No sé / No lo sé. | I don't think so. = No lo creo. | It depends. = Depende. |
|---|---|---|---|
| I don't understand. = No entiendo. | Could you please ...? = ¿Podría usted ..., por favor? | Could you please speak more slowly? = ¿Podría usted hablar más lento, por favor? | A bit more slowly, please. = Un poco más lento, por favor. |
| Please spell it. = Deletréela, por favor. | Please write it down.. = Escríbamela, por favor. | Please repeat it. = Repítalo, por favor. | What does this word mean? = ¿Qué significa esta palabra? |
| How old are you? = ¿Cuántos años tiene? / ¿Cuántos años tienes? | What's your age? = ¿Cuál es su edad? | I'm twenty. = Tengo veinte años. | She/he is very young. = Es muy joven. |
| She/he is old. = Es viejo. | | | |

# Match The Animals

Name: _____

Date: _____

Learn how to *look up* words in a *Spanish-English dictionary or online*. Write the corresponding letter(s).

|  | |  | |  |  |
|---|---|---|---|---|---|
| 1 | ☐ | Ant | | el pájaro | A |
| 2 | ☐ | Antelope | | el camaleón | B |
| 3 | ☐ | Bat | | el oso polar | C |
| 4 | ☐ | Bear | | la oveja | D |
| 5 | ☐ | Beaver | | el cangrejo | E |
| 6 | ☐ | Bedbug | | la gallina | F |
| 7 | ☐ | Bee | | el antílope | G |
| 8 | ☐ | Bird | | el lince | H |
| 9 | ☐ | Bison | | la gaviota | I |
| 10 | ☐ | Boar | | la serpiente | J |
| 11 | ☐ | Buffalo | | la onza | K |
| 12 | ☐ | Bull | | el gorrión | L |
| 13 | ☐ | Butterfly | | el sapo | M |
| 14 | ☐ | Calf | | el burro | N |
| 15 | ☐ | Camel | | el pulpo | O |
| 16 | ☐ | Carp | | el pingüino | P |
| 17 | ☐ | Cat | | el tiburón | Q |

|  | | | | | |
|---|---|---|---|---|---|
| 18 | ☐ | Chameleon | el lucio | R |
| 19 | ☐ | Chamois | el búfalo | S |
| 20 | ☐ | Cheetah | el cabrito | T |
| 21 | ☐ | Chicken | el ternero | U |
| 22 | ☐ | Chimpanzee | el gato | V |
| 23 | ☐ | Cock | el castor | W |
| 24 | ☐ | Cockroach | el lobo | X |
| 25 | ☐ | Cow | el mosquito | Y |
| 26 | ☐ | Crane | el cocodrilo | Z |
| 27 | ☐ | Crayfish | el delfín | AA |
| 28 | ☐ | Cricket | el bisonte | AB |
| 29 | ☐ | Crocodile | la langosta | AC |
| 30 | ☐ | Cuckoo | la ardilla | AD |
| 31 | ☐ | Deer | el arenque | AE |
| 32 | ☐ | Dog | el perro | AF |
| 33 | ☐ | Dolphin | la trucha | AG |
| 34 | ☐ | Donkey | el pollo | AH |
| 35 | ☐ | Dove | la panda | AI |
| 36 | ☐ | Duck | el león | AJ |
| 37 | ☐ | Eagle | la raya | AK |
| 38 | ☐ | Elephant | el toro | AL |
| 39 | ☐ | Falcon | el topo | AM |

| # | | English | | Spanish | Code |
|---|---|---|---|---|---|
| 40 | ☐ | Ferret | | el erizo | AN |
| 41 | ☐ | Fish | | el corzo | AO |
| 42 | ☐ | Fly | | el pelícano | AP |
| 43 | ☐ | Foal | | el ciervo volante | AQ |
| 44 | ☐ | Fox | | el águila | AR |
| 45 | ☐ | Frog | | la nutria | AS |
| 46 | ☐ | Giraffe | | la gamuza | AT |
| 47 | ☐ | Gnat | | el ratón | AU |
| 48 | ☐ | Goat | | el conejo | AV |
| 49 | ☐ | Goose | | el salmón | AW |
| 50 | ☐ | Gorilla | | el oso | AX |
| 51 | ☐ | Guinea Pig | | la jirafa | AY |
| 52 | ☐ | Gull | | el lagarto | AZ |
| 53 | ☐ | Hamster | | el tigre | BA |
| 54 | ☐ | Hedgehog | | el grillo | BB |
| 55 | ☐ | Hen | | la rata | BC |
| 56 | ☐ | Herring | | el jabalí | BD |
| 57 | ☐ | Hippo | | el colibrí | BE |
| 58 | ☐ | Horse | | la carpa | BF |
| 59 | ☐ | Hummingbird | | la tortuga | BG |
| 60 | ☐ | Hyena | | el paro | BH |
| 61 | ☐ | Jackal | | el faisán | BI |

| # | | English | | Spanish | Code |
|---|---|---|---|---|---|
| 62 | ☐ | Jaguar | | el búho | BJ |
| 63 | ☐ | Jellyfish | | la golondrina | BK |
| 64 | ☐ | Kangaroo | | la víbora | BL |
| 65 | ☐ | Kid | | el jaguar | BM |
| 66 | ☐ | Lion | | el piojo | BN |
| 67 | ☐ | Lizard | | la mariposa | BO |
| 68 | ☐ | Lobster | | el chinche | BP |
| 69 | ☐ | Locust | | el caracol | BQ |
| 70 | ☐ | Louse | | el cuco | BR |
| 71 | ☐ | Lynx | | el estornino | BS |
| 72 | ☐ | Mare | | el loro | BT |
| 73 | ☐ | Mole | | la cebra | BU |
| 74 | ☐ | Mouse | | la medusa | BV |
| 75 | ☐ | Nightingale | | la avispa | BW |
| 76 | ☐ | Octopus | | el pavo | BX |
| 77 | ☐ | Ostrich | | la alondra | BY |
| 78 | ☐ | Otter | | el hipopótamo | BZ |
| 79 | ☐ | Owl | | el bogavante | CA |
| 80 | ☐ | Oyster | | la cigüeña | CB |
| 81 | ☐ | Panda Bear | | el halcón | CC |
| 82 | ☐ | Panther | | el gallo | CD |
| 83 | ☐ | Parrot | | el pato | CE |

| # | | English | | Spanish | Code |
|---|---|---|---|---|---|
| 84 | ☐ | Peacock | ● la araña | CF |
| 85 | ☐ | Pelican | ● el cerdo | CG |
| 86 | ☐ | Penguin | ● el cuervo | CH |
| 87 | ☐ | Pheasant | ● el caballo | CI |
| 88 | ☐ | Pig | ● la hiena | CJ |
| 89 | ☐ | Piglet | ● el canguro | CK |
| 90 | ☐ | Pike | ● el murciélago | CL |
| 91 | ☐ | Polar Bear | ● el escorpión | CM |
| 92 | ☐ | Pony | ● el cochinillo | CN |
| 93 | ☐ | Rabbit | ● la abeja | CO |
| 94 | ☐ | Raccoon | ● la garrapata | CP |
| 95 | ☐ | Rat | ● la cobaya | CQ |
| 96 | ☐ | Raven | ● el calamar | CR |
| 97 | ☐ | Ray Fish | ● el avestruz | CS |
| 98 | ☐ | Rhinoceros | ● la grulla | CT |
| 99 | ☐ | Roe | ● la cabra | CU |
| 100 | ☐ | Salmon | ● el poni | CV |
| 101 | ☐ | Scorpion | ● el pavón | CW |
| 102 | ☐ | Seal | ● la oca | CX |
| 103 | ☐ | Shark | ● el camello | CY |
| 104 | ☐ | Sheep | ● el cisne | CZ |
| 105 | ☐ | Skylark | ● la rana | DA |

| # | | English | | Spanish | Code |
|---|---|---|---|---|---|
| 106 | | Sloth | | el perezoso | DB |
| 107 | | Snail | | el ruiseñor | DC |
| 108 | | Snake | | el elefante | DD |
| 109 | | Sparrow | | el gorila | DE |
| 110 | | Spider | | el hámster | DF |
| 111 | | Squid | | el chimpancé | DG |
| 112 | | Squirrel | | la hormiga | DH |
| 113 | | Stag Beetle | | el zorro | DI |
| 114 | | Starling | | el pez | DJ |
| 115 | | Stork | | el atún | DK |
| 116 | | Swallow | | el chacal | DL |
| 117 | | Swan | | la ostra | DM |
| 118 | | Tadpole | | la pantera | DN |
| 119 | | Tick | | el renacuajo | DO |
| 120 | | Tiger | | la foca | DP |
| 121 | | Tit | | el mapache | DQ |
| 122 | | Toad | | el potro | DR |
| 123 | | Trout | | la cucaracha | DS |
| 124 | | Tuna | | la paloma | DT |
| 125 | | Turkey | | el ciervo | DU |
| 126 | | Turtle | | el rinoceronte | DV |
| 127 | | Viper | | la ballena | DW |

| 128 | ☐ | Wasp | la mosca | DX |
| 129 | ☐ | Whale | la vaca | DY |
| 130 | ☐ | Wolf | el hurón | DZ |
| 131 | ☐ | Zebra | la yegua | EA |

Pick 10 animal Spanish words from above and work on arranging them in order alphabetically:

Name: _____

Date: _____

# Countries

Learn how to *look up* words in a *Spanish-English dictionary or online*. Carefully choose the correct Spanish spelling for each of the countries listed below.

1. Algeria
    a. Algerie'
    b. Argelia

2. Armenia
    a. Armenia
    b. Armeeia

3. Azerbaijan
    a. Azerbaiyán
    b. Azerarijan

4. Belarus
    a. Belarús
    b. Belarus

5. Belgium
    a. Belgcum
    b. Bélgica

6. Bosnia and Herzegovina
    a. Bosnia-Herzegovina
    b. Bosnua and Herzegolina

7. Brazil
    a. Brazils
    b. Brasil

8. Bulgaria
    a. Bulgariaz
    b. Bulgaria

9. Cambodia
    a. Kambodia
    b. Cambodia

10. Canada
    a. Canadia
    b. Canadá

11. Cape Verde
    a. Caeo Verde
    b. Cabo Verde

12. Central African Republic
    a. República Centroafricana
    b. Central Akrican Republic

13. China
    a. Chinia
    b. China

14. Colombia
    a. Colombiaz
    b. Colombia

15. Croatia
    a. Croacia
    b. Croatiaz

16. Cyprus
    a. Chipre
    b. Cyprus

17. Czech Republic
    a. Czech Republia
    b. República Checa

18. Denmark
    a. Dinamarca
    b. Denmarka

19. Egypt
    a. Egipto
    b. Egyptz

20. England
    a. England
    b. Inglaterra

21. Estonia
    a. Estonia
    b. Estonias

22. Finland
    a. Finlandia
    b. Finland

23. France
    a. Francia
    b. Francie

24. Georgia
    a. Georgia
    b. Georgiaz

25. Germany
    a. Alemania
    b. Germany

26. Greece
    a. Greecia
    b. Grecia

27. Hungary
    a. Hungría
    b. Hungarin

28. Iceland
    a. Islandia
    b. Iceland

29. Ireland
    a. Irelanda
    b. Irlanda

30. Italy
    a. Italia
    b. Italy

31. Ivory Coast
    a. Costa de Marfil
    b. Ivory Coasta

32. Japan
    a. Japón
    b. Japans

33. Kazakhstan
    a. Kazajstán
    b. Kauakhstan

34. Kyrgyzstan
    a. Kirquistán
    b. Kyroyzstan

35. Latvia
    a. Letonia
    b. Latviain

36. Lebanon
    a. Líbano
    b. Lebanon

37. Lithuania
    a. Lituania
    b. Lithuanio

38. Luxembourg
    a. Luxembourg
    b. Luxemburgo

39. Malaysia
    a. Malaysian
    b. Malasia

40. Maldives
    a. Maldives
    b. Maldivas

41. Mauritius
    a. Mauritiuos
    b. Mauritania

42. Morocco
    a. Moroccoz
    b. Marruecos

43. Netherlands
    a. Países Bajos
    b. Netherlandzo

44. New Zealand
    a. Zealand Newio
    b. Nueva Zelanda

45. North Korea
    a. Koreaian
    b. Corea del Norte

46. Norway
    a. Noruega
    b. Norwayio

47. Papua New Guinea
    a. Papua Guinea
    b. Papúa Nueva Guinea

48. Philippines
    a. Philippinnaos
    b. Filipinas

49. Poland
    a. Polonia
    b. Polandingo

50. Portugal
    a. Portugalz
    b. Portugal

51. Romania
    a. Rumanía
    b. Romonia

52. Russia
    a. Russian
    b. Rusia

53. Scotland
    a. Scotlandizo
    b. Escocia

54. Serbia and Montenegro
    a. Serbiaoz Montunegro
    b. Serbia y Montenegro

55. Slovakia
    a. Slovakio
    b. Eslovaquia

56. Slovenia
    a. Slovenion
    b. Eslovenia

57. South Africa
    a. Sudáfrica
    b. South Africaino

58. South Korea
    a. Corea del Sur
    b. South Koreao

59. Spain
    a. Spainio
    b. España

60. Swaziland
    a. Swazilanduo
    b. Swazilandia

61. Sweden
    a. Swedeni
    b. Suecia

62. Switzerland
    a. Switzerlando
    b. Suiza

63. Taiwan
    a. Taiwán
    b. Taiwanuoi

64. Tajikistan
    a. Tayikistán
    b. Tajikistanuo

65. Thailand
    a. Tailandia
    b. Thailand

66. Tunisia
    a. Tunisio
    b. Túnez

67. Turkey
    a. Turquía
    b. Turkeio

68. Ukraine
    a. Ucrania
    b. Ukraino

69. United Kingdom
    a. United Kingdom
    b. Reino Unido

70. United States
    a. United States
    b. Estados Unidos

71. Vatican City
    a. Ciudad del Vaticano
    b. VatiUan City

72. Wales
    a. Gales
    b. Walesio

Name: _____

Date: _____

# Languages & Nationalities

Learn how to *look up* words in a *Spanish-English dictionary or online. Carefully c*hoose the correct Spanish spelling for each of the entities listed below.

1. Albanian
    a. albanés
    b. escocés

2. Arabian
    a. finés
    b. árabe

3. Bosnian
    a. bosnio
    b. sueco

4. Bulgarian
    a. búlgaro
    b. español

5. Chinese
    a. chino
    b. búlgaro

6. Croatian
    a. alemán
    b. croata

7. Czech
    a. japonés
    b. checo

8. Danish
    a. danés
    b. inglés

9. Dutch
    a. escocés
    b. holandés

10. English
    a. inglés
    b. ruso

11. Estonian
    a. estonio
    b. noruego

12. Finnish
    a. español
    b. finés

13. French
    a. polaco
    b. francés

14. German
    a. alemán
    b. griego

15. Greek
    a. polaco
    b. griego

16. Hebrew
    a. hebreo
    b. croata

**17.** Hungarian
   a. portugués
   b. húngaro

**18.** Irish
   a. checo
   b. irlandés

**19.** Italian
   a. italiano
   b. español

**20.** Japanese
   a. albanés
   b. japonés

**21.** Latvian
   a. búlgaro
   b. letón

**22.** Lithuanian
   a. ucraniano
   b. lituano

**23.** Norwegian
   a. noruego
   b. italiano

**24.** Polish
   a. polaco
   b. escocés

**25.** Portuguese
   a. irlandés
   b. portugués

**26.** Romanian
   a. croata
   b. rumano

**27.** Russian
   a. lituano
   b. ruso

**28.** Scottish
   a. búlgaro
   b. escocés

**29.** Serbian
   a. estonio
   b. serbio

**30.** Slovakian
   a. serbio
   b. eslovaco

**31.** Slovenian
   a. esloveno
   b. italiano

**32.** Spanish
   a. español
   b. irlandés

**33.** Swedish
   a. sueco
   b. hebreo

**34.** Turkish
   a. esloveno
   b. turco

**35.** Ukrainian
   a. polaco
   b. ucraniano

Name: _____

Date: _____

# Match The Pairs - Clothes

Learn how to *look up* words in a *Spanish-English dictionary or online.* Write corresponding letter(s) for the correct answer.

|  | |  | |  |  |
|---|---|---|---|---|---|
| 1 | ☐ | Belt | | el suéter | A |
| 2 | ☐ | Blouse | | el pantalón corto | B |
| 3 | ☐ | Boots | | el camisón | C |
| 4 | ☐ | Button | | el gorro | D |
| 5 | ☐ | Cap | | la manga | E |
| 6 | ☐ | Clothes | | las gafas de sol | F |
| 7 | ☐ | Coat | | el calcetín | G |
| 8 | ☐ | Corduroy | | la ropa | H |
| 9 | ☐ | Cotton | | la seda | I |
| 10 | ☐ | Flannel | | el impermeable | J |
| 11 | ☐ | Gloves | | la pana | K |
| 12 | ☐ | Gown | | la ropa interior | L |
| 13 | ☐ | Hat | | la bufanda | M |
| 14 | ☐ | Jacket | | el esmoquin | N |
| 15 | ☐ | Leather | | el sombrero | O |
| 16 | ☐ | Leisure Suit | | el cuero | P |
| 17 | ☐ | Necktie | | el pantalón | Q |

| # | | English | | Spanish | Code |
|---|---|---|---|---|---|
| 18 | ☐ | Nightdress | | la corbata | R |
| 19 | ☐ | Pajamas | | el bolsillo | S |
| 20 | ☐ | Pocket | | el algodón | T |
| 21 | ☐ | Raincoat | | el pañuelo | U |
| 22 | ☐ | Scarf | | el botón | V |
| 23 | ☐ | Shawl | | las zapatillas | W |
| 24 | ☐ | Shirt | | el abrigo | X |
| 25 | ☐ | Shoes | | la camisa | Y |
| 26 | ☐ | Shorts | | la chaqueta | Z |
| 27 | ☐ | Silk | | los guantes | AA |
| 28 | ☐ | Skirt | | el chaleco | AB |
| 29 | ☐ | Sleeve | | el chándal | AC |
| 30 | ☐ | Slippers | | la bata | AD |
| 31 | ☐ | Socks | | la franela | AE |
| 32 | ☐ | Suit | | el cinturón | AF |
| 33 | ☐ | Sunglasses | | los zapatos | AG |
| 34 | ☐ | Sweater | | la cremallera | AH |
| 35 | ☐ | Trousers | | el traje | AI |
| 36 | ☐ | Tuxedo | | el pijama | AJ |
| 37 | ☐ | Underwear | | la blusa | AK |
| 38 | ☐ | Velvet | | las botas | AL |
| 39 | ☐ | Vest | | la falda | AM |

| 40 | ☐ | Wool | • | • | el terciopelo | AN |
| 41 | ☐ | Zipper | • | • | la lana | AO |

Pick 10 clothes Spanish words from above and work on arranging them in order alphabetically:

# Languages & Nationalities

Name: _____

Date: _____

Learn how to *look up* words in a *Spanish-English dictionary or online. Carefully c*hoose the correct Spanish spelling for each of the entities listed below.

1. Biscuit
    a. la galleta
    b. la canela

2. Bonbon
    a. el bombón
    b. la uva pasa

3. Bratwurst
    a. la sidra
    b. la salchicha

4. Bread
    a. la miel
    b. el pan

5. Bun
    a. el panecillo
    b. la harina

6. Butter
    a. la mantequilla
    b. el chorizo

7. Cake
    a. el bollo
    b. la sal

8. Champagne
    a. el champán
    b. el pescado

9. Cheese
    a. el queso
    b. el yogurt

10. Chocolate
    a. el chocolate
    b. el aceite de oliva

11. Cider
    a. la sidra
    b. el refresco

12. Cinnamon
    a. la canela
    b. el azúcar

13. Cocoa
    a. la miel
    b. el cacao

14. Coffee
    a. la sidra
    b. el café

15. Cream
    a. la pimienta
    b. la nata

16. Egg
    a. el chorizo
    b. el huevo

17. Fish
    a. el cacao
    b. el pescado

18. Flour
    a. la harina
    b. el té

19. Ham
    a. el jamón
    b. el queso

20. Honey
    a. la uva pasa
    b. la miel

21. Ice Cream
    a. el helado
    b. el chorizo

22. Juice
    a. el zumo
    b. la galleta

23. Kefir
    a. la especia
    b. el kéfir

24. Margarine
    a. la uva pasa
    b. la margarina

25. Meat
    a. la miel
    b. la carne

26. Milk
    a. la leche
    b. la miel

27. Milk Powder
    a. la leche
    b. la leche en polvo

28. Mineral Water
    a. el agua mineral
    b. el bombón

29. Mustard
    a. el panecillo
    b. la mostaza

30. Olive Oil
    a. el aceite de oliva
    b. la pimienta

31. Pepper
    a. la pimienta
    b. el aceite de oliva

32. Raisin
    a. el agua mineral
    b. la uva pasa

33. Rice
    a. la canela
    b. el arroz

34. Salt
    a. la sal
    b. la galleta

35. Sausage
    a. el chocolate
    b. el chorizo

36. Soft Drink
    a. el refresco
    b. la miel

**37.** Spice
   a. la especia
   b. la canela

**38.** Sugar
   a. la harina
   b. el azúcar

**39.** Tea
   a. el té
   b. el vinagre

**40.** Vinegar
   a. el arroz
   b. el vinagre

**41.** Water
   a. el agua
   b. el zumo

**42.** Wine
   a. el vino
   b. el cacao

**43.** Yogurt
   a. el yogurt
   b. el cacao


Find 10 other foods that are not listed and write them in English and Spanish:

..................................................................................................................................................................................

..................................................................................................................................................................................

..................................................................................................................................................................................

..................................................................................................................................................................................

..................................................................................................................................................................................

..................................................................................................................................................................................

..................................................................................................................................................................................

..................................................................................................................................................................................

..................................................................................................................................................................................

..................................................................................................................................................................................

# SPORTS

| | | | |
|---|---|---|---|
| Athletics<br>=<br>el atletismo | Badminton<br>=<br>el bádminton | Baseball<br>=<br>el béisbol | Basketball<br>=<br>el baloncesto |
| Boxing<br>=<br>el boxeo | Championship =<br>el campeonato | Chess<br>=<br>el ajedrez | Cup<br>=<br>la copa |
| Cycling<br>=<br>el ciclismo | Discus Throw<br>=<br>el lanzamiento de disco | Draw<br>=<br>el empate | Fencing<br>=<br>la esgrima |
| Football<br>=<br>el fútbol | Gymnastics<br>=<br>la gimnasia | Handball<br>=<br>el balonmano | High Jump<br>=<br>el salto de altura |
| Ice Hockey<br>=<br>el hockey hielo | Javelin Throw =<br>el lanzamiento de jabalina | Long Jump<br>=<br>el salto de longitud | Match<br>=<br>el partido |

| | | | |
|---|---|---|---|
| Pole Vault = el salto con pértiga | Riding = la equitación | Sailing = la vela | Skiing = el esquí |
| Sport = el deporte | Sportsman = el/la deportista | Swimming = la natación | Table Tennis = el tenis de mesa |
| Tennis = el tenis | Volleyball = el voleibol | Water Polo = el waterpolo | |

Find 4 other sports from around the world that is not listed and write them in English and Spanish:

_____

_____

_____

_____

# Fruits & Veggies

Name: _____

Date: _____

Learn how to *look up* words in a *Spanish-English dictionary or online. Carefully* choose the correct Spanish spelling for each of the entities listed below.

1. Almond
    a. la almendra
    b. la guinda

2. Apple
    a. la manzana
    b. el mango

3. Apricot
    a. la uva
    b. el albaricoque

4. Artichoke
    a. la alcachofa
    b. la mandarina

5. Asparagus
    a. el espárrago
    b. el colinabo

6. Aubergine
    a. el melón
    b. la berenjena

7. Avocado
    a. la patata
    b. el aguacate

8. Banana
    a. el aguacate
    b. el plátano

9. Basil
    a. la níspola
    b. la albahaca

10. Bean
    a. el ajo
    b. la judía

11. Blackberry
    a. la zarzamora
    b. el apio

12. Blackthorn
    a. la castaña
    b. la endrina

13. Broccoli
    a. el brécol
    b. la ciruela

14. Brussels Sprouts
    a. el bretón
    b. el aguacate

15. Cabbage
    a. el repollo
    b. la trufa

16. Cantaloupe
    a. el melón
    b. el espárrago

17. Cumin
    a. el saúco
    b. el comino

18. Carrot
    a. la zanahoria
    b. la berenjena

19. Cauliflower
    a. la coliflor
    b. el membrillo

20. Celery
    a. el apio
    b. la zarzamora

21. Cherry
    a. la patata
    b. la cereza

22. Chestnut
    a. la patata
    b. la castaña

23. Chicory
    a. la achicoria
    b. el apio

24. Corn
    a. el repollo
    b. el maíz

25. Cranberry
    a. el arándano
    b. el saúco

26. Cucumber
    a. el mango
    b. el pepino

27. Currant
    a. la grosella
    b. la calabaza

28. Date
    a. la ciruela
    b. el dátil

29. Dill
    a. el tomate
    b. el eneldo

30. Elder
    a. el saúco
    b. la frambuesa

31. Fig
    a. el higo
    b. el saúco

32. Garlic
    a. el comino
    b. el ajo

33. Grape
    a. la uva
    b. el bretón

34. Green Beans
    a. las judías verdes
    b. la patata

35. Green Peas
    a. el guisante
    b. la níspola

36. Green Pepper
    a. el bretón
    b. el pimiento

37. Horse Radish
   a. el rábano picante
   b. la fresa silvestre

38. Kohlrabi
   a. el membrillo
   b. el colinabo

39. Lemon
   a. el limón
   b. la frambuesa

40. Lentil
   a. la lenteja
   b. el ruibarbo

41. Mango
   a. el mango
   b. el escaramujo

42. Medlar
   a. la almendra
   b. la níspola

43. Mushroom
   a. la seta
   b. el colinabo

44. Nut
   a. la manzana
   b. la nuez

45. Orange
   a. el saúco
   b. la naranja

46. Parsley
   a. el perejil
   b. la seta

47. Peach
   a. el melocotón
   b. la piña

48. Pear
   a. la sandía
   b. la pera

49. Pepper
   a. el pepino
   b. la pimienta

50. Pineapple
   a. la piña
   b. la frambuesa

51. Plum
   a. el ajo
   b. la ciruela

52. Potato
   a. el espárrago
   b. la patata

53. Pumpkin
   a. la calabaza
   b. el dátil

54. Quince
   a. el membrillo
   b. la endrina

55. Radish
   a. el rábano
   b. la judía

56. Raspberry
   a. la frambuesa
   b. el higo

57. Rhubarb
    a. el ruibarbo
    b. la fresa

58. Rosehip
    a. el colinabo
    b. el escaramujo

59. Sorrel
    a. la uva
    b. la acedera

60. Sour Cherry
    a. el aguacate
    b. la guinda

61. Spinach
    a. el limón
    b. la espinaca

62. Strawberry
    a. la zanahoria
    b. la fresa

63. Tangerine
    a. la alcachofa
    b. la mandarina

64. Tomato
    a. la grosella
    b. el tomate

65. Truffle
    a. la trufa
    b. el bretón

66. Water Melon
    a. la sandía
    b. la espinaca

67. Wild Strawberry
    a. la fresa
    b. la fresa silvestre


Find 7 other foods that are not listed and write them in English and Spanish:

_____

_____

_____

_____

_____

_____

_____

Name: _____

Date: _____

# Body Parts

Learn how to *look up* words in a *Spanish-English dictionary or online.* Carefully choose the correct Spanish spelling for each of the entities listed below.

1. Ankle
   a. el tobillo
   b. el talón

2. Arm
   a. el brazo
   b. la rodilla

3. Armpit
   a. el muslo
   b. la axila

4. Back
   a. la planta
   b. la espalda

5. Backbone
   a. el intestino
   b. el espinazo

6. Beard
   a. la barba
   b. la ceja

7. Belly
   a. la pestaña
   b. el vientre

8. Blood
   a. el talón
   b. la sangre

9. Body
   a. el talón
   b. el cuerpo

10. Bone
    a. la cintura
    b. el hueso

11. Brain
    a. el músculo
    b. el cerebro

12. Cheek
    a. el ojo
    b. la mejilla

13. Chest
    a. el pecho
    b. la frente

14. Ear
    a. la oreja
    b. el dedo del pie

15. Elbow
    a. el codo
    b. el esqueleto

16. Eye
    a. el codo
    b. el ojo

17. Eyebrow
    a. el índice
    b. la ceja

18. Eyelash
    a. la boca
    b. la pestaña

19. Face
    a. la sien
    b. la cara

20. Finger
    a. la uña
    b. el dedo

21. Fist
    a. el índice
    b. el puño

22. Foot
    a. el pelo
    b. el pie

23. Forefinger
    a. el índice
    b. la sien

24. Forehead
    a. la cara
    b. la frente

25. Hair
    a. la pierna
    b. el pelo

26. Hand
    a. la sien
    b. la mano

27. Head
    a. la cabeza
    b. la cadera

28. Heart
    a. la mejilla
    b. el corazón

29. Heel
    a. la piel
    b. el talón

30. Hips
    a. el vientre
    b. la cadera

31. Intestines
    a. la rodilla
    b. el intestino

32. Kidney
    a. la barba
    b. el riñón

33. Knee
    a. la rodilla
    b. el pecho

34. Leg
    a. la piel
    b. la pierna

35. Lips
    a. la frente
    b. los labios

36. Little Finger
    a. la planta
    b. el dedillo

**37.** Liver
   a. la oreja
   b. el hígado

**38.** Lung
   a. el esqueleto
   b. el pulmón

**39.** Moustache
   a. el bigote
   b. la pierna

**40.** Mouth
   a. la rodilla
   b. la boca

**41.** Muscle
   a. el músculo
   b. el hígado

**42.** Nail
   a. la uña
   b. el riñón

**43.** Neck
   a. la oreja
   b. el cuello

**44.** Nerve
   a. el estómago
   b. el nervio

**45.** Nose
   a. la nariz
   b. la planta

**46.** Occiput
   a. el órgano
   b. la nuca

**47.** Organ
   a. el órgano
   b. el pecho

**48.** Palm
   a. la palma
   b. el ojo

**49.** Ring Finger
   a. el dedo del pie
   b. el dedo anular

**50.** Shoulder
   a. el ojo
   b. el hombro

**51.** Skeleton
   a. el esqueleto
   b. la frente

**52.** Skin
   a. la mejilla
   b. la piel

**53.** Skull
   a. la nuca
   b. el cráneo

**54.** Sole
   a. la planta
   b. el cuerpo

**55.** Stomach
   a. la boca
   b. el estómago

**56.** Temple
   a. la piel
   b. la sien

**57.** Thigh
   a. el muslo
   b. los labios

**58.** Throat
   a. la garganta
   b. el puño

**59.** Thumb
   a. la ceja
   b. el pulgar

**60.** Toe
   a. el hígado
   b. el dedo del pie

**61.** Tongue
   a. la lengua
   b. el hígado

**62.** Tooth
   a. el diente
   b. la espalda

**63.** Waist
   a. la cintura
   b. el puño

**64.** Womb
   a. el útero
   b. el hígado

**65.** Wrist
   a. la muñeca
   b. el bigote

# Business & Economy

Name: _____

Date: _____

Learn how to *look up* words in a *Spanish-English dictionary or online*. Carefully choose the correct Spanish spelling for each of the entities listed below.

1. Assortment
    a. el surtido
    b. la competencia

2. Auction
    a. el superávit
    b. la subasta

3. Auditing
    a. el banco
    b. la auditoría

4. Balance
    a. el capital
    b. el saldo

5. Bank
    a. la mercancía
    b. el banco

6. Bankruptcy
    a. la quiebra
    b. los bienes

7. Business
    a. el negocio
    b. los recursos

8. Capital
    a. el capital
    b. el interés

9. Client
    a. el mercado
    b. el cliente

10. Company
    a. la empresa
    b. la factura

11. Competition
    a. la competencia
    b. el saldo

12. Consumer
    a. el consumidor
    b. los recursos

13. Consumption
    a. el consumo
    b. el índice bursátil

14. Credit
    a. el crédito
    b. el interés

15. Customs
    a. la aduana
    b. la auditoría

16. Debt
    a. la deuda
    b. la demanda

17. Demand
    a. la demanda
    b. el importador

18. Economy
    a. la bolsa
    b. la economía

19. Expenses
    a. los gastos
    b. los bienes

20. Exporter
    a. el pedido
    b. el exportador

21. Fair
    a. la feria
    b. el importador

22. Finances
    a. el capital
    b. las finanzas

23. Foreign Exchange
    a. la competencia
    b. la divisa

24. Goods
    a. la tienda
    b. los bienes

25. Importer
    a. la demanda
    b. el importador

26. Income
    a. el seguro
    b. el ingreso

27. Industry
    a. la industria
    b. el capital

28. Insurance
    a. el seguro
    b. el consumo

29. Interest
    a. el interés
    b. el cliente

30. Invoice
    a. la factura
    b. el dinero

31. Market
    a. el mercado
    b. el consumo

32. Merchandise
    a. el ingreso
    b. la mercancía

33. Money
    a. el surtido
    b. el dinero

34. Order
    a. el lucro
    b. el pedido

35. Price
    a. los gastos
    b. el precio

36. Profit
    a. el lucro
    b. las finanzas

37. Resources
    a. el exportador
    b. los recursos

38. Share
    a. el precio
    b. la acción

39. Shareholder
    a. el/la accionista
    b. la demanda

40. Shop, Store
    a. el dinero
    b. la tienda

41. Stock Exchange
    a. la bolsa
    b. el precio

42. Stock Market Index
    a. el surtido
    b. el índice bursátil

43. Supply
    a. la oferta
    b. el capital

44. Surplus
    a. la quiebra
    b. el superávit

45. Tax
    a. el impuesto
    b. el precio

46. Trade
    a. el comercio
    b. el impuesto

47. Transaction
    a. el consumidor
    b. la transacción

48. Unemployment
    a. el desempleo
    b. el consumidor

# Match Politics Terms

Name: _____
Date: _____

Learn how to *look up* words in a *Spanish-English dictionary or online*. Write the corresponding letter(s).

|  | |  | |  | |
|---|---|---|---|---|---|
| 1 | ☐ | Campaign | | la dictadura | A |
| 2 | ☐ | Candidate | | el golpe de Estado | B |
| 3 | ☐ | Coalition | | el diputado | C |
| 4 | ☐ | Coup | | el gobierno | D |
| 5 | ☐ | Democracy | | la campaña | E |
| 6 | ☐ | Demonstration | | el partido | F |
| 7 | ☐ | Demonstrator | | la libertad de expresión | G |
| 8 | ☐ | Deputy, Representative | | el estado | H |
| 9 | ☐ | Dictatorship | | la oposición | I |
| 10 | ☐ | Diplomacy | | el presidente | J |
| 11 | ☐ | Elections | | el movimiento | K |
| 12 | ☐ | Electoral | | electoral | L |
| 13 | ☐ | Foreign Policy | | el ministerio | M |
| 14 | ☐ | Freedom Of Speech | | el ministro | N |
| 15 | ☐ | Government | | el/la manifestante | O |
| 16 | ☐ | Internal Affairs | | el/la portavoz | P |
| 17 | ☐ | Majority | | la política interior | Q |

|  | |  | |  |  |
|---|---|---|---|---|---|
| 18 | ☐ | Minister | | el voto | R |
| 19 | ☐ | Ministry | | la política exterior | S |
| 20 | ☐ | Minority | | el candidato | T |
| 21 | ☐ | Movement | | el primer ministro | U |
| 22 | ☐ | Opposition | | las elecciones | V |
| 23 | ☐ | Parliament | | el plebiscito/referendo | W |
| 24 | ☐ | Party | | la democracia | X |
| 25 | ☐ | Politician | | la minoría | Y |
| 26 | ☐ | President | | la mayoría | Z |
| 27 | ☐ | Prime Minister | | la manifestación | AA |
| 28 | ☐ | Referendum | | la diplomacia | AB |
| 29 | ☐ | Spokesperson | | la coalición | AC |
| 30 | ☐ | State | | el político | AD |
| 31 | ☐ | Vote | | el parlamento | AE |

Pick 7 politics Spanish words from above and work on arranging them in order alphabetically:

----

----

----

----

----

----

----

SCORE:_____

DATE:--------------------

# Translate

Translate each to English so you can understand the meaning.

| | |
|---|---|
| Dos más dos = <br> English_____ | Cuatro <br> English_____ |
| Tres menos dos = <br> English_____ | Uno <br> English_____ |
| Cinco más diez = <br> English_____ | Quince <br> English_____ |
| Veinte dividido por cuatro = <br> English_____ | Cinco <br> English_____ |
| Treinta menos cinco = <br> English_____ | Veinticinco <br> English_____ |
| Veintidós más ocho = <br> English_____ | Treinta <br> English_____ |
| Veinticinco más dos = <br> English_____ | Veintisiete <br> English_____ |

| | |
|---|---|
| Veintiséis menos dieciséis = <br><br>English_____ | Diez <br><br>English_____ |
| Tres por tres = <br><br>English_____ | Nueve <br><br>English_____ |
| Once más dos = <br><br>English_____ | Trece <br><br>English_____ |
| Catorce más cinco = <br><br>English_____ | Diecinueve <br><br>English_____ |
| Cuatro por siete = <br><br>English_____ | Veintiocho <br><br>English_____ |
| Doce más dieciocho = <br><br>English_____ | Treinta <br><br>English_____ |
| Veintiocho menos ocho = <br><br>English_____ | Veinte <br><br>English_____ |
| Ocho por dos = <br><br>English_____ | Dieciséis <br><br>English_____ |
| Veintisiete dividido por uno = <br><br>English_____ | Veintisiete <br><br>English_____ |

Date: _____

# Fun Idioms You Might Know

Download the free **Google Translate** app. Select the conversation option via the app. Speak each English word or phrase into your device. You'll *hear* the *translation* spoken aloud in Spanish as well written in Spanish. Write down the Spanish version for each below.

- As easy as ABC
  - _____
  - _____

- Call it a day
  - _____
  - _____

- Fell on deaf ears
  - _____
  - _____

- Raining cats and dogs
  - _____
  - _____

- Down to the wire
  - _____
  - _____

- Get cold feet
  - _____
  - _____

- Get a kick out of it
  - _____
  - _____

- Busy as a bee
  - _____
  - _____

- Cross your fingers
  - _____
  - _____

- Cool as a cucumber
  - _____
  - _____

- Crack a book
  - _____
  - _____

- Giving the cold shoulder
  - _____
  - _____

- Fill in the blanks
  - _____
  - _____

- Cat got your tongue?
  - _____
  - _____

- I'm all ears
  - _____
  - _____

- A little birdie told me
  - _____
  - _____

- It cost an arm and a leg
  - _____
  - _____

- Put a bug in his ear
  - _____
  - _____

- Have a change of heart
  - _____
  - _____

- Play it by ear
  - _____
  - _____

- Let the cat out of the bag
  - _____
  - _____

- See eye to eye
  - _____
  - _____

- Mixed feelings
  - _____
  - _____

- Curiosity killed the cat
  - _____
  - _____

- In the same boat
  - _____
  - _____

- Get off your high horse
  - _____
  - _____

- Miss the boat
  - _____
  - _____

- Cry crocodile tears
  - _____
  - _____

- Wolf in sheep's clothing
  - _____
  - _____

- Get your act together
  - _____
  - _____

- Hold your horses
  - _____
  - _____

- Give it a shot
  - _____
  - _____

- Night owl
  - _____
  - _____

- Have second thoughts
  - _____
  - _____

- In hot water
  - _____
  - _____

- I've got your number
  - _____
  - _____

- Slipped my mind
  - _____
  - _____

- Mumbo jumbo
  - _____
  - _____

- Out of the blue
  - _____
  - _____

- Pass with flying colors
  - _____
  - _____

- Read between the lines
  - _____
  - _____

- The icing on the cake
  - _____
  - _____

- Speak your mind
  - _____
  - _____

- Piece of cake
  - _____
  - _____

- Second to none
  - _____
  - _____

*Write down the Spanish subtitles while watching TV*

**Switch your TV or device to Spanish subtitles... so you can match the Spanish words with the spoken English.**

See how many Spanish subtitles can you capture while watching TV.

## *Boost your food vocabulary*
# Write your grocery and household shopping list in Spanish.

Make a dedicated list of the foods or items you or someone plan to buy at the store.

No matter how much time you spend studying Spanish, you must have lots of conversations to become conversationally fluent.

Spend the next several weeks doing a mix of things such as - texting, chatting online, writing emails and talking all in Spanish.

Use the next 10 sheets in this book to track your experience.

Write Date & Type of Activity (texting, email, talking, etc)

**Did you learn any new words? Write them here.**

Write some or all of the things you spoke or wrote in Spanish today.

Write Date & Type of Activity (texting, email, talking, etc)

Did you learn any new words? Write them here.

Write some or all of the things you spoke or wrote in Spanish today.

Write Date & Type of Activity (texting, email, talking, etc)

Did you learn any new words? Write them here.

Write some or all of the things you spoke or wrote in Spanish today.

Write Date & Type of Activity (texting, email, talking, etc)

Did you learn any new words? Write them here.

Write some or all of the things you spoke or wrote in Spanish today.

**Write Date & Type of Activity (texting, email, talking, etc)**

**Did you learn any new words? Write them here.**

**Write some or all of the things you spoke or wrote in Spanish today.**

Write Date & Type of Activity (texting, email, talking, etc)

Did you learn any new words? Write them here.

Write some or all of the things you spoke or wrote in Spanish today.

Write Date & Type of Activity (texting, email, talking, etc)

Did you learn any new words? Write them here.

Write some or all of the things you spoke or wrote in Spanish today.

**Write Date & Type of Activity (texting, email, talking, etc)**

**Did you learn any new words? Write them here.**

**Write some or all of the things you spoke or wrote in Spanish today.**

Write Date & Type of Activity (texting, email, talking, etc)

Did you learn any new words? Write them here.

Write some or all of the things you spoke or wrote in Spanish today.

Write Date & Type of Activity (texting, email, talking, etc)

Did you learn any new words? Write them here.

Write some or all of the things you spoke or wrote in Spanish today.

Another way to learn new Spanish vocabulary is to label all of the items that you see every day with small post-it notes.

For example; computer, stove, mirror, microwave, TV, shoes, door, wall, bed, chair, table, printer, pillow, washing machine, game console, phone, pictures, etc.

Now go on and create some Spanish post-it-notes!

# Spelling Test

| | **Your Answers** | | **Correct Spelling If Incorrect** |
|---|---|---|---|
| 1 | | 1 | |
| 2 | | 2 | |
| 3 | | 3 | |
| 4 | | 4 | |
| 5 | | 5 | |
| 6 | | 6 | |
| 7 | | 7 | |
| 8 | | 8 | |
| 9 | | 9 | |
| 10 | | 10 | |
| 11 | | 11 | |
| 12 | | 12 | |
| 13 | | 13 | |
| 14 | | 14 | |
| 15 | | 15 | |
| 16 | | 16 | |
| 17 | | 17 | |
| 18 | | 18 | |
| 19 | | 19 | |
| 20 | | 20 | |

# Spelling Test

| **Your Answers** | | **Correct Spelling If Incorrect** |
|---|---|---|
| 1 | | 1 |
| 2 | | 2 |
| 3 | | 3 |
| 4 | | 4 |
| 5 | | 5 |
| 6 | | 6 |
| 7 | | 7 |
| 8 | | 8 |
| 9 | | 9 |
| 10 | | 10 |
| 11 | | 11 |
| 12 | | 12 |
| 13 | | 13 |
| 14 | | 14 |
| 15 | | 15 |
| 16 | | 16 |
| 17 | | 17 |
| 18 | | 18 |
| 19 | | 19 |
| 20 | | 20 |

# Spelling Test

| | **Your Answers** | | **Correct Spelling If Incorrect** |
|---|---|---|---|
| 1 | | 1 | |
| 2 | | 2 | |
| 3 | | 3 | |
| 4 | | 4 | |
| 5 | | 5 | |
| 6 | | 6 | |
| 7 | | 7 | |
| 8 | | 8 | |
| 9 | | 9 | |
| 10 | | 10 | |
| 11 | | 11 | |
| 12 | | 12 | |
| 13 | | 13 | |
| 14 | | 14 | |
| 15 | | 15 | |
| 16 | | 16 | |
| 17 | | 17 | |
| 18 | | 18 | |
| 19 | | 19 | |
| 20 | | 20 | |

# Spelling Test

| **Your Answers** | **Correct Spelling If Incorrect** |
|---|---|
| 1 | 1 |
| 2 | 2 |
| 3 | 3 |
| 4 | 4 |
| 5 | 5 |
| 6 | 6 |
| 7 | 7 |
| 8 | 8 |
| 9 | 9 |
| 10 | 10 |
| 11 | 11 |
| 12 | 12 |
| 13 | 13 |
| 14 | 14 |
| 15 | 15 |
| 16 | 16 |
| 17 | 17 |
| 18 | 18 |
| 19 | 19 |
| 20 | 20 |

# Spelling Test

| | Your Answers | | Correct Spelling If Incorrect |
|---|---|---|---|
| 1 | | 1 | |
| 2 | | 2 | |
| 3 | | 3 | |
| 4 | | 4 | |
| 5 | | 5 | |
| 6 | | 6 | |
| 7 | | 7 | |
| 8 | | 8 | |
| 9 | | 9 | |
| 10 | | 10 | |
| 11 | | 11 | |
| 12 | | 12 | |
| 13 | | 13 | |
| 14 | | 14 | |
| 15 | | 15 | |
| 16 | | 16 | |
| 17 | | 17 | |
| 18 | | 18 | |
| 19 | | 19 | |
| 20 | | 20 | |

# Spelling Test

| **Your Answers** | | **Correct Spelling If Incorrect** |
|---|---|---|
| 1 | | 1 |
| 2 | | 2 |
| 3 | | 3 |
| 4 | | 4 |
| 5 | | 5 |
| 6 | | 6 |
| 7 | | 7 |
| 8 | | 8 |
| 9 | | 9 |
| 10 | | 10 |
| 11 | | 11 |
| 12 | | 12 |
| 13 | | 13 |
| 14 | | 14 |
| 15 | | 15 |
| 16 | | 16 |
| 17 | | 17 |
| 18 | | 18 |
| 19 | | 19 |
| 20 | | 20 |

# Spelling Test

| **Your Answers** | | **Correct Spelling If Incorrect** |
|---|---|---|
| 1 | | 1 |
| 2 | | 2 |
| 3 | | 3 |
| 4 | | 4 |
| 5 | | 5 |
| 6 | | 6 |
| 7 | | 7 |
| 8 | | 8 |
| 9 | | 9 |
| 10 | | 10 |
| 11 | | 11 |
| 12 | | 12 |
| 13 | | 13 |
| 14 | | 14 |
| 15 | | 15 |
| 16 | | 16 |
| 17 | | 17 |
| 18 | | 18 |
| 19 | | 19 |
| 20 | | 20 |

# Spelling Test

| **Your Answers** | | **Correct Spelling If Incorrect** |
|---|---|---|
| 1 | | 1 |
| 2 | | 2 |
| 3 | | 3 |
| 4 | | 4 |
| 5 | | 5 |
| 6 | | 6 |
| 7 | | 7 |
| 8 | | 8 |
| 9 | | 9 |
| 10 | | 10 |
| 11 | | 11 |
| 12 | | 12 |
| 13 | | 13 |
| 14 | | 14 |
| 15 | | 15 |
| 16 | | 16 |
| 17 | | 17 |
| 18 | | 18 |
| 19 | | 19 |
| 20 | | 20 |

# Spelling Test

| **Your Answers** | | **Correct Spelling If Incorrect** |
|---|---|---|
| 1 | | 1 |
| 2 | | 2 |
| 3 | | 3 |
| 4 | | 4 |
| 5 | | 5 |
| 6 | | 6 |
| 7 | | 7 |
| 8 | | 8 |
| 9 | | 9 |
| 10 | | 10 |
| 11 | | 11 |
| 12 | | 12 |
| 13 | | 13 |
| 14 | | 14 |
| 15 | | 15 |
| 16 | | 16 |
| 17 | | 17 |
| 18 | | 18 |
| 19 | | 19 |
| 20 | | 20 |

# Spelling Test

| **Your Answers** | | **Correct Spelling If Incorrect** |
|---|---|---|
| 1 | | 1 |
| 2 | | 2 |
| 3 | | 3 |
| 4 | | 4 |
| 5 | | 5 |
| 6 | | 6 |
| 7 | | 7 |
| 8 | | 8 |
| 9 | | 9 |
| 10 | | 10 |
| 11 | | 11 |
| 12 | | 12 |
| 13 | | 13 |
| 14 | | 14 |
| 15 | | 15 |
| 16 | | 16 |
| 17 | | 17 |
| 18 | | 18 |
| 19 | | 19 |
| 20 | | 20 |

# Spelling Test

| **Your Answers** | | **Correct Spelling If Incorrect** |
|---|---|---|
| 1 | | 1 |
| 2 | | 2 |
| 3 | | 3 |
| 4 | | 4 |
| 5 | | 5 |
| 6 | | 6 |
| 7 | | 7 |
| 8 | | 8 |
| 9 | | 9 |
| 10 | | 10 |
| 11 | | 11 |
| 12 | | 12 |
| 13 | | 13 |
| 14 | | 14 |
| 15 | | 15 |
| 16 | | 16 |
| 17 | | 17 |
| 18 | | 18 |
| 19 | | 19 |
| 20 | | 20 |

# Spelling Test

| **Your Answers** | | **Correct Spelling If Incorrect** |
|---|---|---|
| 1 | | 1 |
| 2 | | 2 |
| 3 | | 3 |
| 4 | | 4 |
| 5 | | 5 |
| 6 | | 6 |
| 7 | | 7 |
| 8 | | 8 |
| 9 | | 9 |
| 10 | | 10 |
| 11 | | 11 |
| 12 | | 12 |
| 13 | | 13 |
| 14 | | 14 |
| 15 | | 15 |
| 16 | | 16 |
| 17 | | 17 |
| 18 | | 18 |
| 19 | | 19 |
| 20 | | 20 |

## TRACK YOUR GRADES & AREAS YOU NEED TO WORK ON

| Week | Monday | Tuesday | Wednesday | Thursday | Friday |
|---|---|---|---|---|---|
| 1 | | | | | |
| 2 | | | | | |
| 3 | | | | | |
| 4 | | | | | |
| 5 | | | | | |
| 6 | | | | | |
| 7 | | | | | |
| 8 | | | | | |
| 9 | | | | | |
| 10 | | | | | |
| 11 | | | | | |
| 12 | | | | | |
| 13 | | | | | |
| 14 | | | | | |
| 15 | | | | | |
| 16 | | | | | |
| 17 | | | | | |
| 18 | | | | | |

**Notes**

## TRACK YOUR GRADES & AREAS YOU NEED TO WORK ON

| Week | Monday | Tuesday | Wednesday | Thursday | Friday |
|---|---|---|---|---|---|
| 1 | | | | | |
| 2 | | | | | |
| 3 | | | | | |
| 4 | | | | | |
| 5 | | | | | |
| 6 | | | | | |
| 7 | | | | | |
| 8 | | | | | |
| 9 | | | | | |
| 10 | | | | | |
| 11 | | | | | |
| 12 | | | | | |
| 13 | | | | | |
| 14 | | | | | |
| 15 | | | | | |
| 16 | | | | | |
| 17 | | | | | |
| 18 | | | | | |

**Notes**

Please let us know if something is incorrect.

You can report errors in this book to reportbookerrors@gmail.com.

Thank you.

Made in United States
Orlando, FL
28 July 2023